The No Bullshit Guide

to

Novel Writing

By

Mark Gordon

"An excellent, no-nonsense approach to writing a novel."

- Nicholas J Ordinans

Contents

Introduction

I'm guessing that if you have read beyond the title it's because you want to write a novel, or have at least one manuscript sitting in a drawer somewhere, or a Word document saved to the desktop of your computer. Here's the thing, though. Readers can't read your mind and they generally won't read an unfinished work, although it does happens in some circumstances (more about that later). So, if you want people reading your story and enjoying it, you will need to begin writing and then finish that sucker one way or the other. This book will give you the desire, strategies and personal mindset necessary to get your novel completed to the best of your ability.

The knowledge I acquired by publishing my first novel was extensive, but I did it the hard way. I wish there had been a book like this for me when I started my writing journey, because it would have saved me a lot of heartache and wasted time. I am publishing this information because I know it will be useful to you, no matter where your work sits on the writing continuum. How do I know? I know because I lived it. By reading this book you may avoid some of the simple traps I fell into, that either reduced my writing time or stopped my book from being published faster. Either way, you win.

The book is designed to be read in any order you wish, although there is some logic to the chapter selections. The advice provided is intended to be practical in nature, and I've kept things brief so you can spend more time on your own work. You will find tips in this book that may surprise you by their simplicity. Many of them will sound like simple common sense, yet I don't remember seeing them in the 'serious' creative writing books that I read when I was looking for guidance as a writer.

To authors who may look at this title and scoff because I don't have a degree in English Literature or Creative Writing, I say "I'm fine with that." The book's not for you, anyway. It's for people like me and you - book lovers who think they might just have a novel in them, if they themselves a chance.

So read on, and use these tips as motivation to do what I have done. It's not as hard as you think.

Chapter One

Brutal Facts That Will Make You a Better Writer

Writing is a great thing to do for a whole bunch of reasons, but it's a tough gig. That skinny beatnik hunched over a vintage Olivetti might look like the coolest thing since Salinger created Holden Caulfield, but you can bet he's staring at that blank page with an expression that resembles a deer in the headlights. If you write, you risk it all. You're letting people inside your head and some of those people will be batshit crazy. Here are some things you need to know about being a writer. You may not want to hear them, but it's not my job to tell you that you're amazing and everything will be fine, so here we go.

1. Nobody Cares

Okay, that's not completely true but it got your attention, right? What I'm suggesting here is that people that you expect to care about your passion, won't. Why? Because while you're emptying your soul onto that blank page or into the hard drive of your laptop, all your husband/wife/boyfriend/girlfriend/mother/father sees is someone indulging in a private passion that doesn't include them, so they think you're being selfish and indulgent. Is that a problem? No, because that's just the way writing is. You think Stephen King's wife got pissed occasionally while he was banging out 'Carrie' on that typewriter in the boiler room of their double-wide every night? She might have preferred him to be changing diapers. Thank god he followed his own instincts, though, otherwise I wouldn't have had all that fun reading his books. Oh, and now their baby is all grown up and writing pretty good stories too (Joe Hill), it's obvious that having a dirty diaper didn't ruin his life!

2. Thoughts Count For Nothing

Why don't people understand how amazing you are? You constantly have these really perceptive thoughts and ideas. If only people knew how creative and talented you are. Well, guess what? People aren't mind readers (despite charlatans like John Edwards suggesting otherwise). If you want to communicate your complex, sensitive and meaningful thoughts to others, you need to do it through language. So unless you want to be a singer, a politician or that guy with one shoe who rants on the street corner, you will need to do some writing at some point - actual written words in the language of your choice! Now. Go. Do it.

3. Writing Is Boring

Remember that beatnik hunched over his Olivetti looking all sexy and existential? Well, unfortunately that's just a very romantic and deceptive myth perpetuated by writing wannabes. Writing is a slog. Writing is hard work. Writing is a chore. Now, before you all start getting angry and thinking I must be delusional, just listen for a minute. Despite the fact that writing is like digging ditches, let me tell you, *having written* is a wonderful thing. It's worth the slog. To reread something that you've labored over and not find yourself puking at your own words is a really good feeling. So don't feel disheartened if you're surprised by how boring writing can be while you're actually doing it. It's perfectly normal.

4. You Won't Get Rich

Think about all of the people in the world at this moment who are writing as an occupation, as a hobby or as an obsession. Now, make a list of all the writers who are rich. Say, making a million dollars a year or more. Take your time, I'll wait. Now, work out the odds of becoming rich as a writer. Depressed yet? Well, don't be. Why? Because if you're writing to become rich, you're either insane, twelve years old, or Stephen King's son. Thinking about all the money you might make if your book goes viral is pointless and distracting. You are far better off writing something that you find interesting, and do the best job you can. If your story is honest, engaging and well told you will find an audience. That's all you should be concerned about. If it goes viral then that's just a bonus. Don't put yourself under unrealistic pressure.

5. The Hard Work Starts When You're Done

Have you just finished that 500 page thriller that captures everything that's wrong with post-modern America in a entertaining and dramatic way? Don't put your feet up just yet hotshot, because if you actually want people to read your masterpiece the next part of the journey may be the hardest part. Why? Because now you need to edit that monster, try to find a publisher, market your book, and do everything you can to make sure that your literary baby does not wither and die before it becomes known to the general populace. And why is this so hard? Because you write! Marketing and publicity are skills you probably don't have. Sorry. You're going to need help and time with this one.

Now, why will knowing these brutal facts make you a better writer? Simply because if you continue to write knowing the difficult truth of what's lies before you as a writer, you're doing it for the right reasons. I would probably like to read the stuff you write, because it's going to be honest, thoughtful and will get me into the head of somebody who doesn't simply want to become a literary whore. In other words, I will want to hear what you have to say, and so will others.

So just remember, writing is a slog, but it's worth the effort.

Chapter Two

Ten Things to Help You Succeed as a Writer

Hey, I could be really obvious here and just tell you to write, right? But I'm guessing if you want some actual, practical, useful advice that might get you off your ass and onto the page, then I should try to offer more.

I have recently completed my first novel "Desolation Boulevard" (published through Smashwords) and I can tell you that it's a pretty amazing feeling hold a 500-page book in your hands that you created from scratch. And now a confession - I'm a lazy writer. Really. I needed some strategies to get me through to the end of "Boulevard", but I finished it and people seem to be enjoying it, so I must have done something right. So here are my tips to help you get your writing onto the page and into the ebook store.

1. Turn Off That TV (or iPad or Halo 4 tournament)!

It's a total time waster! For every repeat of Friends that you watch, you could be churning out a page of great prose, which is getting you closer to your goal. Go on. Do it now. Turn off those distractions.

2. Make a Start

This one seems obvious, but it's harder than you think. If you never start, though, you'll never finish, and all great journeys begin with a single step. So, before you clean the house, or eat breakfast or wash the car, get something written. Start that chapter! You'll be amazed how at quickly the words begin to flow. Think about it! Would you rather have a published novel, or a clean car?

3. Trust Your Own Writing Method

Fans of "Desolation Boulevard" often ask me how I knew what to write, and I always reply that I had no idea where the story would lead. When I started Chapter 1, the *only* idea I had was that most of the world's population would go into an unexplained hibernation and wake up as some kind of zombie. That's it. Really. There was no planning and no concept as to how the story might evolve or conclude. I wrote the book in a purely linear fashion, one chapter at a time, mostly not even knowing what was going to happen in the next chapter. That worked for me, but if you need to plan, then plan. Everyone's different.

4. Don't Sweat the Small Stuff

If you get hung up on plot issues or small details like words that don't seem adequate, just keep going. You can always come back later and fix them, after you've had a chance to relax and think. Some of the best solutions to my plot problems came when I wasn't even thinking about my writing. They would just pop into my head later, like magic. Awesome!

5. Let the Story Have a Life of Its Own

You might be writing the story, but guess what? You don't own it. It belongs to itself and eventually the reader. Sometimes things happen that will surprise even the author. I'm currently working on the sequel to my first novel, and I shocked myself quite a bit when I killed off one of my favourite characters just a few chapters in. I had no intention of doing it, but once that part of the story arrived it seemed the right thing to do, despite me not wanting to lose that character. I have no regrets, though, because the story is king.

6. Be a Brutal Editor of Your Own Work

You *will* write stuff you don't need - unnecessary characters, long descriptive passages that don't advance the story, repetitive sections, or parts that make no sense. You know what to do! Delete them then congratulate yourself. You've just made your story a much more pleasant experience for your reader.

7. Write to Your Own Level

I could never have written Cormac McCarthy's "The Road". It's a stunning work of speculative fiction - frightening, moving, profound and incredibly entertaining. There is not a single wasted phrase in that whole book. The plot is as engaging as hell, and the words have the rhythm of poetry. It's amazing! So not something I could create, but I did write a book I'm proud of nonetheless. My way! And guess what? It's finding an audience. If you work hard, and are true to yourself and the story, your work will find an audience too.

8. Avoid Writer's Block

Finding a particular section of your book difficult to finish? Then leave it! Go on to something else. Start a new chapter, introduce a new character, or even start a whole new book. Stephen King has many stories on the boil at the same time - sometimes they sit around in drawers, ignored for years at a time, until he pulls them out and finishes them. Crime writer Raymond Chandler once described how he overcame his problem of having the story grind to a halt - he would just have a character enter the room wielding a gun! Problem solved.

9. You are a God

As a fiction writer you are a fairly significant deity. You are creating worlds, giving birth to multiple characters and deciding how they live and die. Fun! So feel free to live large. Your characters can be completely different to you. Ever wanted to get into the head of a serial killer? You can do it. Ever wondered what it would be like to be married to a movie star? You can write that book. Disappointed that you'll never visit another planet? Spawn your own in a novel. I wondered what it would be like to turn most of the world's population into violent night-dwelling monsters with a taste for flesh. "Desolation Boulevard" is the result of that thought. It's fun to be a god!

10. Embrace Technology and Social Media

One of the most motivating strategies I found to help me persist with my writing was when I posted a few early chapters of my book on Wattpad - a website for writers. I was blown away by the positive feedback and it really encouraged me to write faster than I had been. Knowing that I now had fans waiting for each chapter really inspired me to keep the story going for them. It was a really extraordinary experience and I appreciate every single reader who posted kind words about the book. Try it, but beware - it's addictive!

Chapter Three

How Do I Start?

If you're one of those writers (like I was) who thought that writing a decent book involved a combination of advanced literary technique, ridiculous amounts of planning and an almost mystical gift in the word arts, you might be pleasantly surprised by what I have to share with you. If you have a library full of personal journals outlining your future novel that includes a chapter-by-chapter breakdown of the story and detailed character outlines, that's fine, but this chapter is probably not for you. If you have always wanted to write a novel but thought it was a task best left to others with madder skills, then pay attention. This is for you. What I won't do in this article, though, is teach you how to write. I'll assume that you have some competence in literacy and are capable of stringing a few tasty sentences together occasionally. So, if we agree on those parameters, let's get on with it.

1. Create a Starting Point for Your Story

Now, I realise that some of you will be thinking that this is something that is extremely important and that you couldn't possibly begin your masterpiece without having an amazing idea to work from that has never been done before, but I think you're wrong. A good novel can have any starting point. Not knowing where your story will end up is a really poor excuse to not begin. As I have said in a previous chapter, once your story starts rolling along it will magically begin to assume a life of its own. One incident will lead to another and your characters will start behaving like real people, sometimes in ways that even you don't expect. It's really quite fascinating.

So to prove that beginning your story is actually quite easy, I've invented some scenarios off the top of my head that I believe would evolve quite naturally into full-blown novels.

A man leaves his office for lunch and spies his wife in a cafe with a man he has never seen before.

A parcel arrives in the post to the wrong address, and when it's accidentally opened it contains photos that suggest somebody has been murdered.

Driving into the countryside to begin a career as a teacher in a small country town, a woman picks up hitchhiker who begins to behave oddly.

Despite being happily married with children, a woman meets a man at a party and finds herself drawn to him.

Two teenagers are the only viewers in a cinema, when the movie stops and the lights go out.

Now these ideas are neither very original nor earth-shattering, but the point is they are a place to start. I made them up with very little effort, and feel confident that I could turn any of them into a pretty exciting novel. By the way, at this point in the process I wouldn't even know what genre these stories might be. I guess that would depend on what I felt like writing. This is exactly how I began with "Desolation Boulevard".

2. Keep Your Chapters Short

I think this is really good advice for the first time novelist for a couple of reasons.

Firstly, it breaks down a fairly major task into manageable chunks. Remember that old riddle about achieving your goals? How do you eat an elephant? One mouthful at a time! Writing a novel is a bit like that. By keeping the chapters short (my suggestion would be 1000 - 2000 words) you will see yourself making progress and won't become overwhelmed. Before you know it you'll have ten or twenty chapters done and feel like you're flying along.

Secondly, short chapters are very ebook friendly. Now that the sale of ebooks is outpacing paper books it means that people are reading novels on their portable devices in all kinds of places when they have a few moments to spare. Short chapters really suit this kind of reading. You'll notice I wasn't so obvious as to say young people have shorter attention spans these days. I wanted to, though.

3. Don't Over-Write

I don't mean keep your novel short. I'm saying that you don't need to go crazy with flowery language and super-detailed descriptive passages. Just tell the story. The beauty of a book is that the reader can bring your vision to life using his or her own imagination. You don't need to say:

"Bill wiped the salty sweat from his handsome face and peered into the murky distance as he waited impatiently for his stunningly beautiful wife to disembark from the bus as if being disgorged from the mouth of a whale, like an exotic, fragile sea creature."

Just say:

"Bill flicked sweat from his brow as his wife stepped from the bus. His heart raced."

Or something like that. 200 pages filled with unnecessary adjectives will drive a discerning reader crazy.

4. A Word on Editing

Editing your work is very important, but I believe you need some time before you start changing things radically. I think it's best to leave a completed chapter alone for at least a day or two before you start rereading it, looking to make improvements. There will be a lot of rewriting needed before you release your novel to the public, so you really don't need to worry too much about editing at all when you're in first draft mode. The main thing is to keep taking consistent bites of that "elephant" by writing. Edit when you reach a mental block or can't write any more that day. But don't edit stuff you've just written. You need to leave it for a while so that you can read it as the reader might. It's surprising how you forget things you've written even after just a few days.

5. Another Word on Chapters

A chapter should be like a little story of its own. The best way to get a feel for this is by paying attention to how other authors do it. Find a novel with short chapters and check it out. After a while writing this way becomes second nature.

6. Finishing Your Book

I think there are as many ways to finish a book as there are to begin them. It will all depend on the tone you want to create and the mood you want to leave the reader in. All of the textbooks on writing would be talking about resolution here, but I don't know enough about that. I only know what I did. When I reached a point where I felt like I was getting towards the conclusion of "Desolation Boulevard" I did what I had done throughout the rest of the book. I wrote one chapter at a time and let the story decide on the end point. I like the way my story ended, too, even though I had no idea how it would conclude even when I was just five or six chapters from finishing. I like writing that way, it's fun, and it worked for me.

Chapter Four

Five Tips for Creating Memorable Characters

1. Don't Waste Time on and Unnecessary Backstory

Creating a complex backstory for every character in your book is a waste of time in some situations (if you're not Annie Proulx for example). Your readers have an imagination and will be able to fill in gaps if necessary. Think about it! Do you need to know the life story of every person you meet in your life? Of course not! You don't need to and don't want to, right? Novels are the same. When a character is introduced, all the reader really needs to know is how he or she is relevant to the plot or to other characters. Their actions will usually illustrate motivation as the story develops, which is enough for the reader to be able to join the dots. In other words, back off.

2. Let the Action Reveal the Character

I've received some great feedback about my novel "Desolation Boulevard" but the comments that surprised me the most were the ones that said how much they liked the characters and how believable they were. Why was I surprised? Simply because I spent very little time describing the characters when they were introduced into the story. Rather, I let them loose and allowed them to react to situations based on how I imagined them to be in my mind. In other words, I had an idea of the type of person they were and their actions followed accordingly. The reader could then visualise the character by superimposing their own conceptions and ideas onto them.

3. Don't Over-Describe

Unless it's relevant to the story, do you really need to describe every physical characteristic of every character in your book? I don't know about you, but I get bored when reading overly detailed descriptions of characters. Try this experiment - think of one of your favourite characters from a novel. Now, do you visualise them a certain way because of the way the author described them, or did you just get a vague idea of their appearance based on their behaviour and actions and by using your imagination? Be honest.

4. Let Your Characters Live Their Own Lives

Your characters must not adhere to your personal philosophies and beliefs. That's not how the world is and readers will get bored with bland, clichéd characters quicker than you would believe. For example, if you're a Christian, don't have all of your characters behave like a bunch of morally upright clones. How about creating a character that is an atheist, or even someone who doesn't give a shit either way. It will create conflict, new plot twists and stop you from getting bored. You characters should not be little versions of you. Seriously.

5. Don't Get Attached

Characters are not real people. You have created them and you can make them disappear. They are words on a page and you are god. If your story is more compelling for the death of a character then kill them! Not only will it be incredibly engaging for the reader, but by creating a new, dynamic, plot development you will spawn a whole range of jumping off points that might not even be possible if that character were to live. Precious? Get out of here!

Chapter Five

How To Publish Your Own Work For Zero Cost

If you are a writer you should be considering how you might develop your hobby into a profession. Wouldn't it be fantastic to live the life of a full-time writer? Roll out of bed whenever you like, write for a few hours, stroll down to the local cafe or tavern for a leisurely lunch with a good book, then home for a nap before editing your morning's work in the evening. Sounds good doesn't it? Well, it's only possible if you're willing to live in extreme poverty, or make enough money from your writing to sustain that jolly pleasant lifestyle. So how do you self-publish your work for zero cost so that your work is in the same marketplace as Rowling, Meyer, Tolkien and me? The answer is surprisingly simple - and it's free, despite the fact that many online publishing services will try to charge you up to thousands of dollars for the exact same service. I know because I'm currently being targeted by a number of publishers who are trying to charge me for something I've already done myself, for no cost. They are so keen to get my business, in fact, that they are offering packages for the sequel to my novel, "Desolation Boulevard", despite the fact that it is still only a work in progress. So, as a public service announcement for all of you writers who thought that publishing your work was expensive, here is how it's done.

Option 1: Smashwords Publishing

Many of you have probably heard of Smashwords as a place where you can buy ebooks, but did you know they provide an amazing service that allows you to publish your work online for no costs up front? Here's how it works - after you finish your masterpiece (which could be anything from a novel to a cookbook with photographs), you format your book according to the guidelines provided by Smashwords, then submit it for publication through them. Now, here is the great part - after you have satisfied the formatting requirements (they provide a free ebook to help you through that process) Smashwords will transform your book into all of the main ebook formats such as mobi, pdf, epub etc. and publish it on your behalf to most of the major online booksellers such as Kobo, iTunes, Barnes and Noble, Diesel and the Smashwords online store. Also, as part of the process your book will be given an ISBN number for free, something than many online publishing companies will charge you for. Once your book is published (usually in just a few days) it will begin to appear on the previously mentioned bookstores' websites. Depending on the store, royalties (around 30% mostly) for each book sold will be taken each time one is sold.

Option 2. Amazon CreateSpace

I found out about this one after I had already published through Smashwords, but I went ahead and published a second time because when you publish through Smashwords you retain the copyright of your own work and can do whatever you like with it. The Amazon

CreateSpace works in a very similar way, providing a formatted ebook that goes on sale almost immediately in the Amazon and Kindle stores. The really exciting part of this service, however, is that it enables you to have a print version of your book available online at the Amazon store for no up front costs. As a customer orders your paperback through Amazon, they print up a copy and post it. Genius. Again, for this service CreateSpace takes a very fair royalty for each book sold - I have had sales people from other companies try to charge me thousands of dollars for similar services elsewhere.

So there you go. I believe they are the best two options for self-publishing. If you are interested in how your book will look in an online store compared to, say, the latest Stephen King story, head to any of the ebook stores mentioned above and search for my novel "Desolation Boulevard". It will give you a good idea of what you might expect when you publish your own work.

I did it and so can you.

Chapter Six

Five Facts About Famous Authors That Will Make You Feel Better About Your Own Work

If you're a writer you are probably a little awestruck by the incredible achievements of bestselling authors or writers of the classics. The following facts may put their achievements into perspective and inspire you to persist with your writing, even when you feel you aren't good enough.

1. Leo Tolstoy Hated "War and Peace"

One of the greatest novels of all time was considered to be less than perfect by its famous Russian author. In 1871 Tolstoy wrote in a letter: "I am so happy … that I won't have to write trifles like 'War and Peace' any more".

The lesson: sometimes you are not the best person to judge your own work. Let the audience decide.

2. "Moby Dick" Sold Less Than 3000 Copies

Yes, that's right. The most well known novel of all time - usually also considered to be the best - was met with a very lukewarm response on its' initial release, selling less than 3000 copies. The author, Herman Melville, was so distraught that his next novel was a story about a bitter writer whose novel was unsuccessful.

The lesson: Be patient. Often it takes time for your story to find its' audience.

3. Most of Hemingway's Work Was Shit

Ernest Hemingway, author of "The Old Man and the Sea, "The Green Hills of Africa" and "The Sun Also Rises", wrote only 500 words a day, usually in the morning, and would often finish his writing session halfway through a sentence. He said of his own work: "I write one page of masterpiece to 91 pages of shit. I try to put the shit in the wastebasket."

The lesson: Be a brutal editor of your own work, but write something every day.

4. Harper Lee Wrote Only One Book

It's difficult to believe, but the author of America's most loved novel, "To Kill a Mockingbird" wrote only one book. In 1960 she published "To Kill a Mockingbird" - a sprawling tale of love, strength of family, intolerance, racism and justice that manages to shine a light into the dark recesses of the American psyche, but also one which ends up delivering a poignant message that makes you glad to be a member of the human race. Despite beginning a couple more books, Lee decided not to finish them and they were never published.

The lesson: Your first novel might be your masterwork - it may already be lurking within you, waiting to be released to an appreciative audience. Go for it. There is no "right" time.

5. John Grisham Was Rejected By 28 Different Publishers

The bestselling author of legal thrillers, such as "The Firm" and "The Pelican Brief", was rejected by every major publishing house (and quite a few minor ones as well). His first novel, "A Time To Kill", received an initial print run of only 5000 copies when it was eventually published in 1989. The day after it was published he began working on his second novel, "The Firm", which would go on to sell 47 million copies worldwide. Grisham was working for a law firm full-time, so to get his writing done he would get out of bed at 5am and write for a couple of hours before going to work.

The Lesson: Find time for your writing and be persistent. And remember - the publishers don't always get it right!

Chapter Seven

How To Think Like A Writer

1. Start Calling Yourself a Writer

If you are writing, you are a writer. I was in a bar one afternoon having a quiet drink and the bartender asked me what I did for a living. I thought for a second then, told him I was a writer (rather than tell him my actual paid occupation). He was impressed and asked what I had written. I told him about my novel, "Desolation Boulevard" and gave him a business card that had information about how to purchase the book online. He then asked for extras to hand out to customers. If I told him I was an art teacher, that small marketing opportunity would have been lost. Tell people you are a writer, and you will even start to convince yourself that you are.

2. Get Business Cards Printed.

Whether you are writing blogs, poetry, movie reviews or epic horror novels like me, you want to reach an audience. Now, business cards might be an "old school" way of promoting yourself, but they not only legitimise your work in the eyes of potential readers, but can point them in the direction of your writing, without you having to scramble around for a pen and paper or, even worse, rely on someone's memory. Carry them with you at all times and when the conversation drifts around to your writing, you can politely invite people to check out your work by giving them one of your cards.

3. Avoid Critics!

When you are working on drafts, it's tempting to try to get some positive feedback from work colleagues, friends or family to keep you motivated. Be careful how you do this, though. Harsh criticism from a well-meaning acquaintance can have you second-guessing yourself to the point where your original vision becomes lost and the words stop flowing. This is especially important if you are authoring a longer work such as a novel. Wait until your story is big enough and ugly enough to look after itself, then you may feel comfortable asking for advice. Make a resolution, though, to never give an unfinished novel to a colleague to read, unless you have complete faith in them to be supportive and constructive. If you feel you must go down the path of asking for criticism, you should consider doing it through an online forum for writers where they will understand what you are going through and offer genuine advice based on their own experience. But remember! Never post all of your work online where it can be plagiarised!

4. Write Every Day

You knew this one was coming, didn't you? I can already hear some of you making excuses about the baby that needs changing, or that wedding you have to get ready for, or the housework that needs to be done, but wait a minute! Writing every day doesn't mean a whole new chapter or a short story - it may just be a journal entry or an idea for a new article. Even if it's your wedding day, surely you can spend five or ten minutes writing about what the day means to you. Who knows? It may become inspiration for a best seller one day.

5. Set a Deadline

How many of you have no idea when your work will be finished? I thought so. Started your novel? Excellent. I applaud your ambition. Now, do something really radical - pick a date when you should be finished and stick to it. "How will I know that?" I can hear you asking. Do what I did - work it out. Let's assume you want to write a romance novel of eighty thousand words. That's only one thousand words a day for eighty days. Can't do one thousand words a day? How about five hundred words a day? Okay, now you're up to one hundred and sixty days. Even factoring in days where you won't get a whole chapter done, it's still well under half a year. Easy! Once you've worked out your deadline date, announce it to people with confidence. "My new novel will be finished by October" (or whatever). You think that won't motivate you? Try it.

Chapter Eight

The Best Kept Secret in Writing

Here is the one writing tip above all others that may just get you to the end of your novel. It is simple and profound, yet I have only come to realise its significance recently myself. I don't remember hearing about it in any of my high school English classes, and when it is mentioned in creative writing courses and books, I don't believe it is stressed enough, especially for beginning authors.

Here it is.

Are you ready?

You first draft is allowed to be crap.

Here it is again, in case you missed it.

You first draft is allowed to be crap.

Now, I don't know why this isn't more widely known, but all budding writers should be told this until they get sick of hearing it. Why? Because, it is the one thing that allows you the freedom to keep going with your story, even when you know it's not perfect. That's right! The sinking feeling writers have when they know they are not doing a terribly good job is perfectly normal. In fact, it's almost a prerequisite for being an author.

Producing an average first draft is usually how it's done.

Now, don't get me wrong here. I'm not saying write poorly. Nor am I saying that your story will be awful (that's possible, though). What I'm saying is that your first effort will have many, many flaws. But that's fine. We all create imperfect first drafts, and so will you. The trick is to keep going. Get that story down any way you can, and worry about perfecting it later. That's why we edit.

You don't believe me? One of the world's greatest authors, Ernest Hemingway, once said, *"The first draft of anything is shit."*

So, write. Let the words come and if you can't write the perfect phrase, write an average one just to keep your story going. You can perfect it later.

So, there it is. The most important writing secret. I wish someone had told me about that when I was much younger. I would have been less worried about not creating perfection, and just created.

Remember!

You first draft is allowed to be crap.

Afterword

So that's it.

All you have to do now is sit down and start putting words on a page. I started this writing caper later than most, and I'm angry with myself that I did. If I started twenty years ago I could have had a whole shelf full of novels finished by now.

DON'T PUT IT OFF!

Writing, like any other activity you care to think of, can become a habit, and that's what you need. A habit. You can do it, and it's definitely easier than you think, and much less destructive than crack. An English journalist, Julie Burchill, once said, *"anyone with two brain cells can write a novel."* I'm proof of that, because I'm almost sure I have two brain cells and I have written multiple novels.

I've enjoyed sharing some of my writing experiences with you and I hope you get a sense from this book that writing is not the mystical art it's often portrayed as, even though a well written book is a magical thing.

I wish you all the best with your endeavours and I look forward to seeing your work in print. Let me know how you do.

About the Author

Mark Gordon lives and writes in Newcastle, Australia and became a fan of apocalyptic horror after watching the Omega Man on television as an eleven year old. He has worked as a nightclub operator, disc jockey, photographer, band manager, construction worker, and high school teacher. He has just released the sequel to "Desolation Boulevard", titled "Diamond Creek Dogs".

www.desolationboulevard.net

Cover Design by Mark Holdsworth

www.ingramcontent.com/pod-product-compliance
Lightning Source LLC
Chambersburg PA
CBHW060348290526
45791CB00004B/1581